Contents

T0344323

Scope and Sequence

Welcome

Vocabulary	**Colours:** red, yellow, green, blue **Numbers:** one, two, three, four, five, six, seven, eight, nine, ten **Classroom actions:** sit down, stand up, look, listen, count, open your book, close your book, wave goodbye		**Quest item:** egg
Structures	Hello, I'm (Oscar). My name's (Oscar). His/Her name's (Oscar). His/Her (backpack) is blue.		

1 My birthday

Vocabulary	**Colours:** brown, white, pink, black, orange, purple **Actions:** clap, stamp, jump, walk, run, dance, hop, climb **CLIL (Science):** bird, fish, flower, leaf, butterfly		**CLIL:** Science (Colours in nature) **Wider World:** Birthdays **Phonics: a, p, s, t** (at, sat, pat, tap) **Values:** It's good to share. **Quest item:** blanket
Structures	What's your name? My name is (Millie). How old are you? I'm (seven). What's your favourite colour? My favourite colour is (blue).	Is it (purple)? Yes, it is. / No, it isn't. What colour is it? It's (pink). It's a (butterfly).	

2 At school

Vocabulary	**Classroom objects:** book, pen, pencil, ruler, rubber, pencil sharpener, pencil case, table, chair, desk **Numbers 11–20:** eleven, twelve, thirteen, fourteen, fifteen, sixteen, seventeen, eighteen, nineteen, twenty **CLIL (Music):** drum, piano, violin, guitar		**CLIL:** Music (Musical instruments) **Wider World:** My School **Values:** Work hard at school. **Phonics: d, i, m, n** (dip, dad, it, sit, man, am, nap, pan) **Quest item:** book
Structures	What is this? It's a (book). It's red. It's a (red) (book).	What are these? They're (pencils). What colour are they? They're (red). How many (pencils) can you see? (Five).	

3 My family

Vocabulary	**Family members:** mum, dad, brother, sister, granny, grandad, friend **Occupations:** vet, pilot, doctor, dancer, cook, farmer, dentist, artist **CLIL (Art):** painting, drawing, collage, sculpture		**CLIL:** Art (Types of art) **Wider World:** Family occupations **Values:** Love your family. **Phonics: c, g, o** (can, cap, cat, gas, dig, on, dog, top) **Quest item:** photo
Structures	This is my brother/sister. How old is he/she? He's/She's (seven).	Is he/she a (vet)? Yes, he/she is. Is he/she an (artist)? No, he/she isn't. He's/She's a (teacher). What does (Jack) want to be?	

4 My body

Vocabulary	**Parts of the body:** body, head, hands, arms, feet, legs, fingers, toes, wings, tail **Clothes:** T-shirt, jumper, trousers, dress, skirt, shoes, socks, hat **CLIL (Social sciences):** a dirty face, clean hands, dirty hands, wash your hands!		**CLIL:** Social sciences (Personal hygiene) **Wider World:** Carnivals around the world **Values:** Be clean. **Phonics: ck, e, k** (kick, sock, pen, pet, ten, neck, kid, kit) **Quest item:** soap
Structures	I've got a (green) (tail). I've got (green) (wings).	He's got (blue) (trousers). She's got a (yellow) (head). She's got (four) (legs). They're (purple). You've got (yellow) (hands).	

5 Pets

Vocabulary	**Pets:** dog, cat, rabbit, mouse, tortoise, parrot, frog, snake, hamster **Adjectives:** big, small, tall, short, long, thin, fat, young, old **CLIL (Science):** bird, chick, kitten, puppy, goose, egg	**CLIL:** Science (Baby animals) **Wider World:** Unusual pets **Values:** Take care of your pets. **Phonics: b, h, r, u** (bag, rug, hot, hat, red, rat, up, cup) **Quest item:** mouse
Structures	What's that? It's a (dog). What are those? They're (hamsters).	
	Have you got a (parrot)? Yes, I have. It's a (small parrot). / No, I haven't. Has he/she got a (parrot)? Yes, he/she has. It's a (small parrot). / No, he/she hasn't. He/She's got a (big dog).	

6 My house

Vocabulary	**At home:** house, living room, kitchen, bedroom, bathroom, garden, window, door **At home:** bed, cooker, fridge, TV, sofa, lamp, bath, sink **CLIL (Social sciences):** shop, library, playground, café, zoo, park	**CLIL:** Social sciences (Public places) **Wider World:** Different homes **Values:** Be tidy. **Phonics: f, ff, l, ll** (fig, fan, off, puff, leg, lap, doll, bell) **Quest item:** bed
Structures	Where's Rita? She's in the kitchen. Where are Waldo and Zak? They're in the bedroom.	
	There's a lamp on the desk. There are two kittens under the sofa.	
	Where do you live? I live in a (house). Do you live in a (house)? Yes, I live in a (house). / No, I live in a (flat).	

7 Food

Vocabulary	**Food:** fruit, cheese, bread, meat, salad, milk, juice, chicken, lemonade, yoghurt **Food:** sandwich, water, chocolate, honey, jelly, vegetables, ice cream, cake **CLIL (Social sciences):** sausages, chips, carrots		**CLIL:** Social sciences (Food) **Wider World:** Packed lunches **Values:** Be polite. **Phonics: j, ss, v, w** (jam, jet, kiss, mess, van, vet, web, wig) **Quest item:** milk
Structures	I like (salad) and (meat). I don't like (bread) and (cheese). What do you want? I want (milk).	Do you like (honey)? Yes, I do. / No, I don't. It's good/bad for me.	

8 I'm excited!

Vocabulary	**Adjectives:** hungry, thirsty, tired, scared, excited **Adjectives:** happy, sad, cold, hot, ill, hurt, angry, bored **CLIL (Science):** a long shadow, a short shadow	**CLIL:** Science (Light and shadow) **Wider World:** Shadow puppets in different cultures **Values:** Respect feelings. Help others. **Phonics: qu, x, y, z, zz** (quiz, quick, box, taxi, yes, yell, zap, zip, buzz, fizz) **Quest item:** torch
Structures	Are you (hungry)? Yes, I am. / No, I'm not.	
	Is he/she (cold)? No he/she isn't. He/She is (hurt). Are they (bored)? Yes, they are. / No, they aren't. They are (excited).	
	(This shadow puppet) is from (China).	

Goodbye

Vocabulary	**Quest items:** egg, blanket, book, photo, soap, mouse, bed, milk, torch	
Structures	Her name's Rita. There's a blanket. Waldo is sad. Has she got blue shoes? How many sandwiches can you see?	Is he happy? Where is the frog? Has he got a parrot? Is it a bird?

Festivals

Halloween: witch, monster, cat, bat, pumpkin
Christmas: Santa, reindeer, sleigh, present
Easter: egg, bunny, chick
Summer fun: sun, sky, tree, flower, bird, grass

Welcome

1  (1:02) **Listen and sing.**

Hello, I'm Millie.

Hello, I'm Oscar.

green

red

LOOK!

Hello.	I'm Oscar.
	My name's Oscar.

I'm = I am   name's = name is

2 (1:03) **Listen and play. Then listen and chant.**

My name's Oscar.
Hello, Oscar!
Hello, hello, hello!

My name's Millie.
Hello, Millie!
Hello, hello, hello!

My name's Rita.
Hello, Rita!
Hello, hello, hello!

My name's Zak.
Hello, Zak!
Hello, hello, hello!

3  **Listen and point. Then listen and repeat.**

Quest! Listen and sing. Then find.
Come with us, come on a quest,
Come on a quest today.
Come with us, come on a quest,
Look for an egg today.
An egg, an egg,
Look for an egg today!

4 **Listen and repeat.**

| one | two | three | four | five |
| six | seven | eight | nine | ten |

5 **Listen and chant.**

One, two, three, four, five,
Six, seven, eight, nine, ten.
Now count again!

6 **1:09** **Listen and match. Then say.**

LOOK!
| His name's Oscar. | His backpack is red. |
| Her name's Rita. | Her backpack is yellow. |

His name's Oscar.
His backpack is red.

Number 1!

7 **Draw and guess.**

Her name's Rita.
Her backpack is yellow.

8  **Listen and repeat.**

a **stand up**

b **sit down**

c **look**

d **listen**

e **count**

f **open your book**

g **close your book**

h **wave goodbye**

9 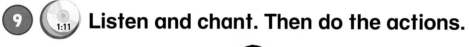 **Listen and chant. Then do the actions.**

Stand up, sit down,
And listen to me.
Open your book
And count to three!

Sit down, stand up,
And look at me.
Close your book
And wave goodbye!

Listen and point. Then play a game.

I can talk about colours. ☐
I can do classroom actions. ☐

1 My birthday

1 1:14 **Listen and point.**

white

brown

pink

2 1:15 **Listen and repeat.**

3 1:16 **Listen and play. Then listen and chant.**

Name, name. What's your name?
Zak, Zak. My name's Zak.
Age, age. How old are you?
Six, six. I'm six.
Colour, colour.
What's your favourite colour?
Blue, blue.
My favourite colour is blue.

black

purple

orange

LOOK!

What's your name?	My name's Millie.
What old are you?	I'm seven.
What's your favourite colour?	My favourite colour is green.

What's = What is   My name's = My name is

4 **Ask and answer.**

What's your name?

How old are you?

What's your favourite colour?

1:17

Quest

Look for a blanket today.
An egg and a blanket!
Look for a blanket today!

5 🎵 1:19 **Listen and repeat.**

a **b** **c** **d** **e** **f** **g** **h**

(clap) (stamp) (jump) (walk) (run) (dance) (hop) (climb)

6 🎵 1:20 **Listen and sing. Then do the actions.** SONG

Happy Birthday!

It's my birthday!
Hip hip hurray! Happy birthday!
Clap, clap, clap.

I'm six today!

It's my birthday!
Hip hip hurray! Happy birthday!
Stamp, stamp, stamp.

I'm seven today!

It's my birthday!
Hip hip hurray! Happy birthday!
Jump, jump, jump.

I'm eight today.

Happy birthday!
Happy birthday!

Cut-outs
p.103

7 **Listen and colour. Then look and circle.**

Is it purple?	Yes, it is. / No, it isn't.
What colour is it?	It's pink.

It's = It is   Isn't = Is not

1

2

3

4

Is it yellow?

Yes, it is. / No, it isn't.

8 **Look and play.**

1

2

3

4

Is it red?

Number 1!

Yes, it is.

10 1:23 **Listen.**

¹ **a**   ² **p**   ³ **s**   ⁴ **t**

11 1:24 **Listen, point and say.**

12 1:25 **Listen and blend the sounds.**

1 a - t   at

2 p - a - t   pat

3 s - a - t   sat

4 t - a - p   tap

13  **Underline _a_, _p_ and _t_. Read the words aloud.**

1 pat

2 tap

14  **Listen and say. Then listen and number.**

a

bird

b

fish `1`

c

flower

d

leaf

e

butterfly

15 **Complete the pictures. Then say.**

1

2
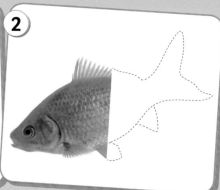

3

4

5

MINI-
PROJECT

Make a poster.
Draw animals
and plants. What
colour are they?

Wider World

A birthday party

16  **Read and trace.**

Hello. My name's Kim. It's my birthday today!

1

Look at my birthday cake! I'm _seven_ .

2

Look at my balloons. My favourite colours are _pink_ and _purple_ .

3

One, two, three, four, five, _six_ presents!

4

Happy _birthday_ to me.

17  **Draw a birthday card for Kim and write.**

1

2

Dear

Love

MINI-PROJECT

Make a birthday chart for your class.

18 **1:30** Listen. Then play.

HAVE FUN!

It's an orange butterfly!

19 **1:31** Listen and do.

Picture Dictionary

AB p.104

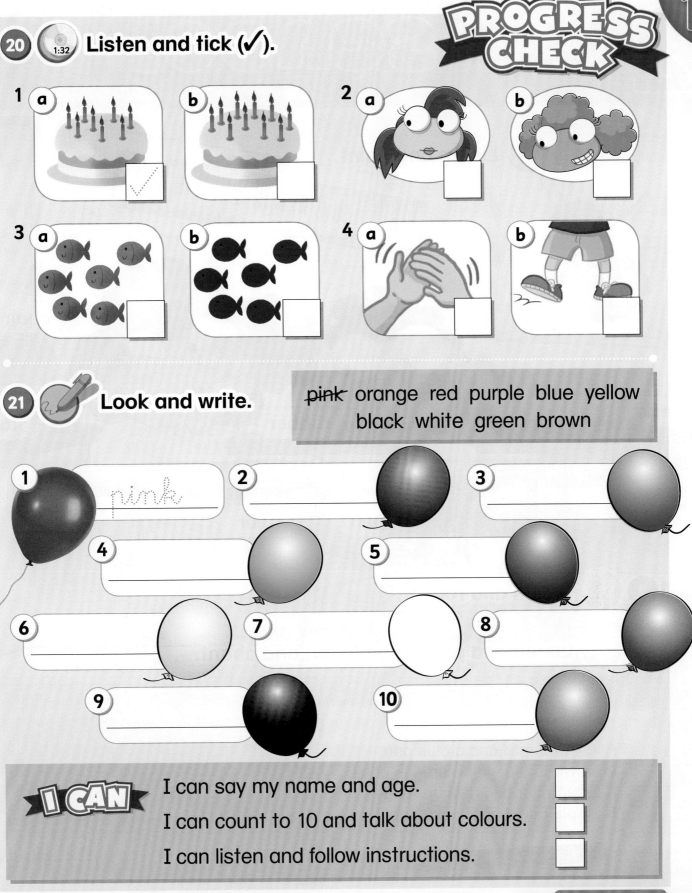

20 1:32 **Listen and tick (✓).**

1 a   b

2 a   b

3 a   b

4 a   b

21 **Look and write.**

~~pink~~ orange red purple blue yellow
black white green brown

1 *pink*   2   3

4   5

6   7   8

9   10

I CAN

I can say my name and age.

I can count to 10 and talk about colours.

I can listen and follow instructions.

2 At school

1 🔊 1:33 **Listen and point.**

desk · chair · rubber · table · pen · ruler

2 🔊 1:34 **Listen and repeat.**

3 🔊 1:35 **Listen and play. Then listen and chant.**

A yellow pencil and a blue pen.
A brown table and an orange chair.
A green ruler and a white rubber.
A purple book. Look, look, look!

LOOK!

| What's this? | It's a book. It's red. It's a red book. |

pencil case

pencil sharpener

book

pencil

4 🔘 1:36 **Listen and number. Then say.**

a

b

c ☐1

d

What's this?

It's a pen. It's yellow.
It's a yellow pen.

🔘 1:37 **Quest**

Look for a book today.
An egg, a blanket and a book!
Look for a book today!

5 🔊 1:39 **Listen and repeat.**

11 eleven

12 twelve

13 thirteen

14 fourteen

15 fifteen

16 sixteen

17 seventeen

18 eighteen

19 nineteen

20 twenty

6 🔊 1:40 **Listen, count and write the numbers. Then sing.**

SONG

Rulers, rulers. How many rulers?
How many rulers can you see?
Hurray! Let's play.
Let's jump and climb. `11`

Books, books. How many books?
How many books can you see?
Hurray! Let's play.
Let's jump and climb.

Pencils, pencils. How many pencils?
How many pencils can you see?
Hurray! Let's play.
Let's jump and climb.

Pens, pens. How many pens?
How many pens can you see?
Hurray! Let's play.
Let's jump and climb.

Rubbers, rubbers. How many rubbers?
How many rubbers can you see?
Hurray! Let's play.
Let's jump and climb.

TIP!
one ruler /
two rulers

Cut-outs ✂ p.105

7   **Listen and circle. Then ask and answer.**

LOOK!

What are these?	They're pencils.
What colour are they?	They're red.
How many pencils can you see?	Five.

They're = They are

2

1
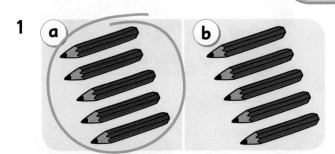

2
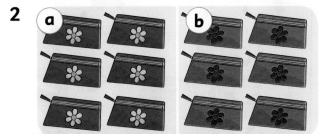

3
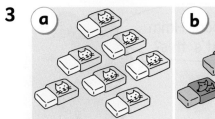 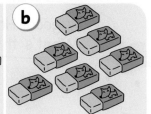

4
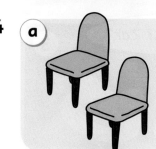 

What are these?

What colour are they?

How many pencils can you see?

They're pencils.

They're red.

Five.

8 **Draw. Then ask and answer.**

SKILLS

1

2

What are these?

They're tables.

9 1:44 **Listen to the story. Then act out.**

 **Work hard at school.**

HOME-SCHOOL LINK

Show your homework to your family.

10 🔘 1:45 **Listen.**

¹ **d**   ² **i**   ³ **m**   ⁴ **n**

11 🔘 1:46 **Listen, point and say.**

12 🔘 1:47 **Listen and blend the sounds.**

1 d - i - p   dip   2 d - a - d   dad

3 i - t   it   4 s - i - t   sit

5 m - a - n   man   6 a - m   am

7 n - a - p   nap   8 p - a - n   pan

13 **Underline *d*, *i*, *m* and *n*. Read the words aloud.**

1 man   2 dip   3 nap

4 pan   5 sit   6 dad

14 (1:51) **Listen and point. Then say.**

1

2

3

piano

violin

4

guitar

drum

15 (1:52) **Listen and number. Then play and say.**

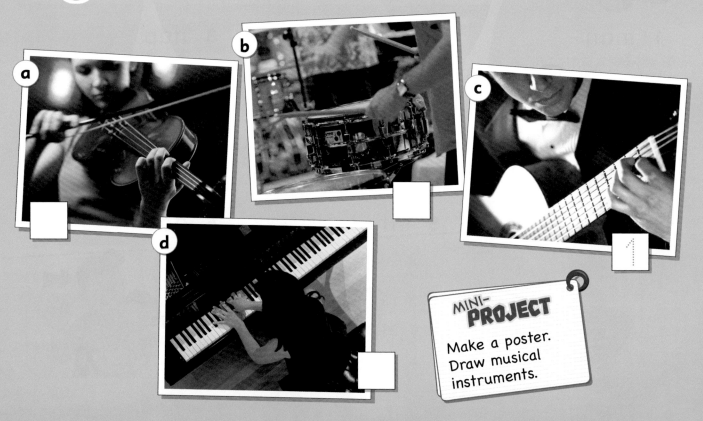

a

b

c

d

MINI-
PROJECT

Make a poster.
Draw musical
instruments.

Wider World

My school

16  **Read and answer.**

> Hello. My name's Alex. Come and see my school.

1

This is my playground. How many pupils can you see?

2

This is my classroom. How many tables can you see? How many chairs? How many books?

3

This is my teacher. Her name's Miss Ellis. What's her favourite colour?

4

This is a science lesson. What colours can you see?

5

My favourite lesson is music. What instruments can you see?

17 **Look at your classroom. Ask and answer.**

> How many pupils can you see?

> What's your teacher's name?

> What's his/her favourite colour?

MINI-PROJECT

Draw a picture of your classroom and write.

19 | 1:54 | Listen and do.

AB p.105

20 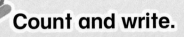 **Count and write.**

pianos drums ~~guitars~~

1

2

3

| 11 | guitars |

21 **Listen and write. Then draw. Listen again and colour.**

ruler pencil case ~~rubbers~~ chairs

1 rubbers

2 _____

3 _____

4 _____

 I can talk about school objects. ☐

I can name musical instruments. ☐

I can use plurals. ☐

3 My family

1 1:56 **Listen and point.**

granny

grandad

friend

brother

2 1:57 **Listen and repeat.**

3 1:58 **Listen and play. Then listen and chant.**

This is me.	This is my brother.	This is my sister.
How old are you?	How old is he?	How old is she?
I'm six, I'm six!	He's one, he's one!	She's eight, she's eight!

LOOK!

This is my brother/sister.

| How old is he/she? | He's/She's nine. |

He's = He is   She's = She is

sister

dad

mum

 4 **1:59** **Listen and write. Then say.**

This is my brother. He's ten.

a

b

c

d

 **1:60 Quest**

Look for a photo today.
An egg, a blanket, a book and a photo!
Look for a photo today!

5 **Listen and repeat.**

TIP!
a vet / an artist.

a vet
b pilot
c doctor
d dancer
e cook
f farmer
g dentist
h artist

6 **Listen, find and match. Then sing and act out.**

SONG

I'm at the airport with my family.
Brother, sister, mum, and dad.
I'm glad, glad, glad.

This is my mum.
She's a pilot.
My dad is a pilot, too.

This is my sister.
She's an artist.
And my brother is a cook.

my sister   my brother   my mum

me   my dad

Cutouts
p.107

7 **Listen and circle. Then ask and answer.**

LOOK!

Is he/she	a vet?	Yes, he/she is.
	an artist?	No, he/she isn't. He's/She's a cook.

1
a   b

2
a   b

3
a   b

4
a   b

Is she a dancer?

No, she isn't. She's an artist.

8 **Look and write.**

pilot vet ~~Is she~~ ~~Yes~~ cook No

1

Is she a teacher?

Yes, she is.

2

Is she a _____?

Yes, she is.

3

Is he a _____?

___, he isn't.

He's a _____.

Listen to the story. Then act out.

 Love your family.

10 1:66 **Listen.**

1

c

2

g

3

o

11 1:67 **Listen, point and say.**

12 1:68 **Listen and blend the sounds.**

1 c - a - n can

2 c - a - p cap

3 c - a - t cat

4 g - a - s gas

5 d - i - g dig

6 o - n on

7 d - o - g dog

8 t - o - p top

13 **Underline c, g and o. Read the words aloud.**

1 dig

2 cap

3 dog

4 on

5 gas

6 can

14  Listen and repeat. Then listen and number.

a

painting

b

collage

c

sculpture

d

drawing

15 Listen and point. Then ask and answer.

a

b

c

d

What's this?

It's a painting.

Is it a dragon?

Yes, it is.

MINI-PROJECT

Make a family portrait. Do a painting, a drawing, a collage or a sculpture!

Wider World

My family

 16 **Read and match. Then write the names.**

a

Jack

b

c

d

1 This is my dad. His name's John. He's a farmer. And this is our farm.

2 This is my mum. Her name's Ann. She's an artist. Look at her painting!

3 My sister is a cook. Her name's Cody. Look at her cakes! Yum!

4 And this is me. My name's Jack. I'm a dancer. Well! I want to be ...

 17 **Read and circle.**

1 Is John a doctor?
Yes, he is. / No, he isn't.

2 Is Cody a cook?
Yes, she is. / No, she isn't.

3 Is Ann a dancer?
Yes, she is. / No, she isn't.

4 What does Jack want to be?
A vet. / A dancer.

MINI- PROJECT

What do you want to be? Draw a picture.

18 (1:75) Listen and point. Then play Os and Xs.

19 (1:76) Listen and act.

He's a doctor.

This is my mum.

AB p.106

20   **Listen and tick (✓).**

1 a    b  ✓   **2** a    b

3 a    b 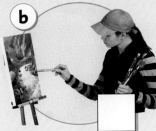   **4** a    b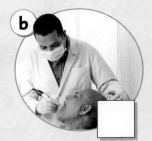

5 a    b    **6** a    b

7 a    b    **8** a    b

 I CAN

I can talk about my family. ☐

I can talk about jobs. ☐

I can talk about art. ☐

4 My body

1 2:01 **Listen and point.**

arms

hands

body

2 2:02 **Listen and repeat.**

3 2:03 **Listen and play. Then listen and chant.**

I've got green arms.
I've got green hands.
I've got green legs.
I've got green feet.

I've got green wings.
I've got a green tail.
I've got a green head,
But now it's red!

5  **Listen and repeat.**

a. T-shirt
b. jumper
c. trousers
d. dress

e. skirt
f. shoes
g. socks
h. hat

6  **Listen and colour the clothes. Then sing.** SONG

I've got a red dress
And a blue hat.
I've got grey socks
And pink shoes.
Stamp your feet with me!
(stamp, stamp)

I've got a green T-shirt
And purple trousers.
I've got a brown jumper
And yellow shoes.
Stamp your feet with me!
(stamp, stamp)

Cut-outs
p.109

7 **Listen and number. Then ask and answer.**

a

b

`1`

c

d

LOOK!

He's got blue trousers.

She's got a yellow head.

She's got four legs.

They're purple.

He's got = He has got
She's got = She has got

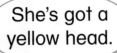

She's got a yellow head.

Number 2!

SKILLS

8 **Colour. Then play.**

a

b

9   **Listen to the story. Then act out.**

10 **2:12** Listen.

1 ck **2 e** **3 k**

11 **2:13** Listen, point and say.

12 **2:14** Listen and blend the sounds.

1 k - i - ck kick   2 s - o - ck sock

3 p - e - n pen   4 p - e - t pet

5 t - e - n ten   6 n - e - ck neck

7 k - i - d kid   8 k - i - t kit

13 Underline *ck*, *e* and *k*. Read the words aloud.

1 pen   2 kid   3 neck

4 sock   5 kick   6 kit

      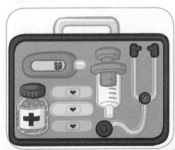

14 2:18 **Listen and number.**

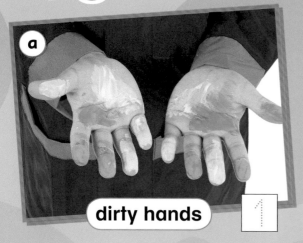

a

dirty hands 1

b

clean hands ☐

c

a dirty face ☐

d

Wash your hands! ☐

15 **Look at Activity 14. Read and write.**

1 I've got dirty hands. _a_

2 And I've got a dirty face! ___

3 Wash your hands. Wash your face. ___

4 I've got clean hands. And I've got a clean face! ___

MINI-**PROJECT**

Make a poster about clean habits.

Wider World

Carnivals around the world

16  **Read and match.**

1
It's carnival time!
There is carnival
music. These are
steel drums. How
many drums can
you see? What
colour are they?

2
Carnival time is
fun. This is me and
my sister.
These are carnival
costumes. I've got
a yellow costume.
I've got a red and
yellow hat.
And I've got a
carnival mask.

3
This is me with my
friends. Can you
see me? I've
got a red and
yellow dress. I've
got red shoes and
black socks.

4
This is a carnival
float. It's a
dragon. He's pink
and green. He's got
green legs. Look at
his teeth!

a

b

c

d

17 **Make a carnival mask!**

1

2

3

4

MINI-PROJECT

Find out about a
carnival in your
country. Make a
poster.

Draw.   **Cut.**   **Colour and stick.**   **Play.**

He's got green wings!

Wash your face!

19 🔘 2:21 **Listen and do.**

Picture Dictionary

AB p.107

20 **2:22** **Listen and number.**

21 **2:23** **Listen and draw.**

1	2	3	4

 I CAN

I can name different parts of the body.

I can talk about clean habits.

I can talk about clothes.

 Family Island

5 Pets

1 2:24 **Listen and point.**

frogs

cat

hamsters

mouse

snakes

2 2:25 **Listen and repeat.**

3 2:26 **Listen and play. Then listen and chant.**

Pets, pets, big and small.
Come and listen to them all.
What's that? It's a parrot. A parrot!
What are those? They're snakes. Snakes!
What's that? It's a dog. A dog!
What are those? They're hamsters. Hamsters!

parrot

tortoise

dog

rabbit

TIP!

one mouse
two mice

LOOK!

| What's that? | It's a dog. |
| What are those? | They're hamsters. |

4 🔊 2:27 **Listen and number. Then ask and answer.**

a b c d e f g h

What's that?

It's a cat.

What are those?

🔊 2:28

They're rabbits.

Look for a mouse today.
An egg, a blanket, a book,
a photo, soap and a mouse!
Look for a mouse today!

5 🔊 2:29 **Listen and repeat.**

a  **big**

b **small**

c **tall**

d **short**

e **long**

f **thin**

g **fat**

h **young**

i **old**

6 🔊 2:30 **Listen and write. Then sing and act.**

SONG

The boy's got a dog,
A very _big_ dog.
He's got a dog. Woof! Woof!

The dog's got a frog,
A very _____ frog.
The dog's got a frog.
Ribbit! Ribbit!

The girl's got a cat,
A very _____ cat.
She's got a cat. Miaow!

The cat's got a hat,
A very _____ hat.
The cat's got a hat. Miaow!

He's got a dog.
The dog's got a frog.
She's got a cat.
And the cat's got a hat!

Cut-outs
p.111

LOOK!

Have you got	a parrot?	Yes, I have. It's a small parrot.
		No, I haven't.
Has he/she got		Yes, he/she has. It's a small parrot.
		No, he/she hasn't. He's/She's got a big dog.

haven't = have not   hasn't = has not

7 2:31 **Listen and write (✓) or (✗). Then ask and answer.**

① ✓   ② ☐   ③ ☐   ④ ☐

Have you got a parrot?

Yes, I have. It's a fat parrot.

8 2:32 **Listen and draw. Then play.**

SKILLS

① ② ③ ④

Has he got a thin hamster?

No, he hasn't. He's got a fat hamster.

Number 1?

Correct!

10 2:35 **Listen.**

1 **b**   **2** **h**   **3** **r**   **4** **u**

11 2:36 **Listen, point and say.**

12 2:37 **Listen and blend the sounds.**

1 b – a – g bag   **2** r – u – g rug

3 h – o – t hot   **4** h – a – t hat

5 r – e – d red   **6** r – a – t rat

7 u – p up   **8** c – u – p cup

13 **Underline b, h, r and u. Read the words aloud.**

1 rat

2 cup

3 rug

4 hat

5 red

6 bag

14  **Listen and repeat. Then match.**

1

cat

2

dog

3

bird

a

chick

b

kitten

c

puppy

15 **Listen and number. Then say.**

a

egg

b

goose

c

chick

MINI-**PROJECT** Make a photo album of baby animals.

Wider World

Unusual pets

16  **Read and circle.**

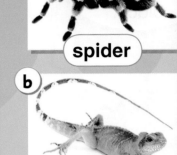

a

spider

b

lizard

My name's Angela. I've got a small pet. It's white and it's got four legs. It's got a long tail. It's a spider / (rat.)

My name's Ben. My pet is small and green. It's got four legs and a tail. It's a lizard / snake.

c

rat

My name's Grace. I've got a small pet. It's black and it's got eight legs. It's a spider / lizard.

My name's Matt. My pet is long and thin. Its red and white. It hasn't got any legs! It's a rat / snake.

d

snake

17 **Ask and answer. Write (✓) or (✗).**

Have you got a spider?

No, I haven't.

MINI-**PROJECT**

Make a class book of unusual pets. Draw and write.

He's got four mice. They're black.

She's got a tortoise. It's green.

1 a  ✓

b

2 a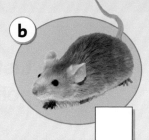

b

3 a

b

4 a

b

5 a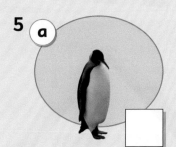

b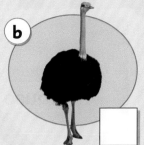

6 a

b

7 a

b

8 a

b

 **I CAN**

I can talk about pets.

I can describe different animals.

6 My house

1 **Listen and point.**

kitchen

living room

house

2 **Listen and repeat.**

3 **Listen and play. Then listen and chant.**

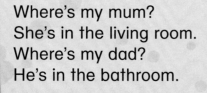

Where's my mum?
She's in the living room.
Where's my dad?
He's in the bathroom.

Where's Rita?
She's in the kitchen.
Where are Waldo and Vava?
They're in the bedroom.

LOOK!

Where's Rita?	She's in the kitchen.
Where are Waldo and Vava?	They're in the bedroom.

Where's = Where is

garden

bedroom

window

door

bathroom

2:50

Quest

Look for a bed today.
An egg, a blanket,
a book, a photo, soap,
a mouse and a bed!
Look for a bed today!

4 2:49 **Listen and write (✓) or (✗). Then say.**

1  ✗

2

3

4

Where's Waldo?

He's in the bathroom.

5 🔘 2:52 **Listen and repeat.**

a **bed**

b **cooker**

c **fridge**

d **TV**

e **sofa**

f **lamp**

g **bath**

h **sink**

6 🔘 2:53 **Listen and write. Then sing.**

SONG

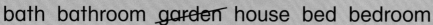

bath bathroom ~~garden~~ house bed bedroom

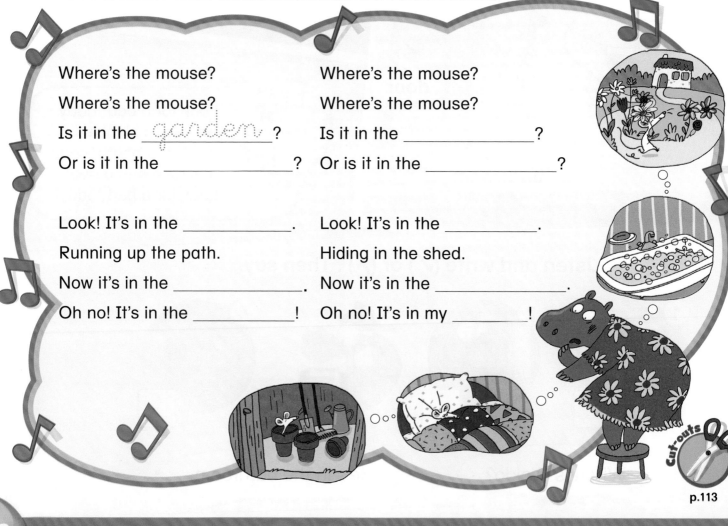

Where's the mouse?

Where's the mouse?

Is it in the _garden_?

Or is it in the _____?

Look! It's in the _____.

Running up the path.

Now it's in the _____.

Oh no! It's in the _____!

Where's the mouse?

Where's the mouse?

Is it in the _____?

Or is it in the _____?

Look! It's in the _____.

Hiding in the shed.

Now it's in the _____.

Oh no! It's in my _____!

Cutouts

p.113

7 **Listen and tick (✓). Then say.**

LOOK!

There's a lamp on the desk.

There are two kittens under the sofa.

There's = There is

TIP!

under

on

in

There's a TV on the cooker.

   8 **Listen and draw. Then play.**

SKILLS

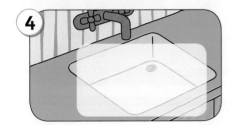

There are two books on the table.

Number 6. My turn.

 Be tidy.

HOME-SCHOOL LINK
Clean your bedroom. Show your family.

64 Lesson 5 story and values (be tidy)

AB p.62

10 Listen.

1 **f** **2** **ff** **3** **l** **4** **ll**

11 Listen, point and say.

12 Listen and blend the sounds.

1 f - i - g fig **2** f - a - n fan

3 o - ff off **4** p - u - ff puff

5 l - e - g leg **6** l - a - p lap

7 d - o - ll doll **8** b - e - ll bell

13 Underline *f*, *ff*, *l* and *ll*. Read the words aloud.

1 leg

2 doll

3 fig

4 puff

5 bell

6 fan

14 **Listen and number. Then say.**

a **shop**

b **library**

c **playground** 1

d **café**

e **zoo**

f **park**

15  **Listen and match.**

1

2

3

4

a

b

c

d

MINI-PROJECT

Draw a picture of yourself in your favourite place.

Wider World
Different homes

16 **Read and match.**

1

My name's Ella. I live in a small house. There is a kitchen, a living room, a bathroom and two bedrooms. I've got a big garden.

a

b

3

My name's Rosie. I live in a caravan! It's small but it's nice. There's a living room, a kitchen and a bathroom.

2

My name's Ravi. I live on a houseboat. It's a big boat. There is a living room and two bedrooms. My favourite room is the living room.

c

d

4

My name's Juan. I live in a big flat. There is a kitchen, a living room, two bathrooms and four bedrooms. I've got a TV in my bedroom.

17 **What about you? Ask and answer.**

Where do you live?

Do you live in a house?

What's your favourite room?

Have you got a TV in your bedroom?

MINI-PROJECT

Draw your home and write about it.

Listen and tick (✓). Then ask and answer.

Where's Zak?

He's in the house.
He's in the kitchen.

  Listen and act.

AB p.109

AB p.66

20 Look and write.

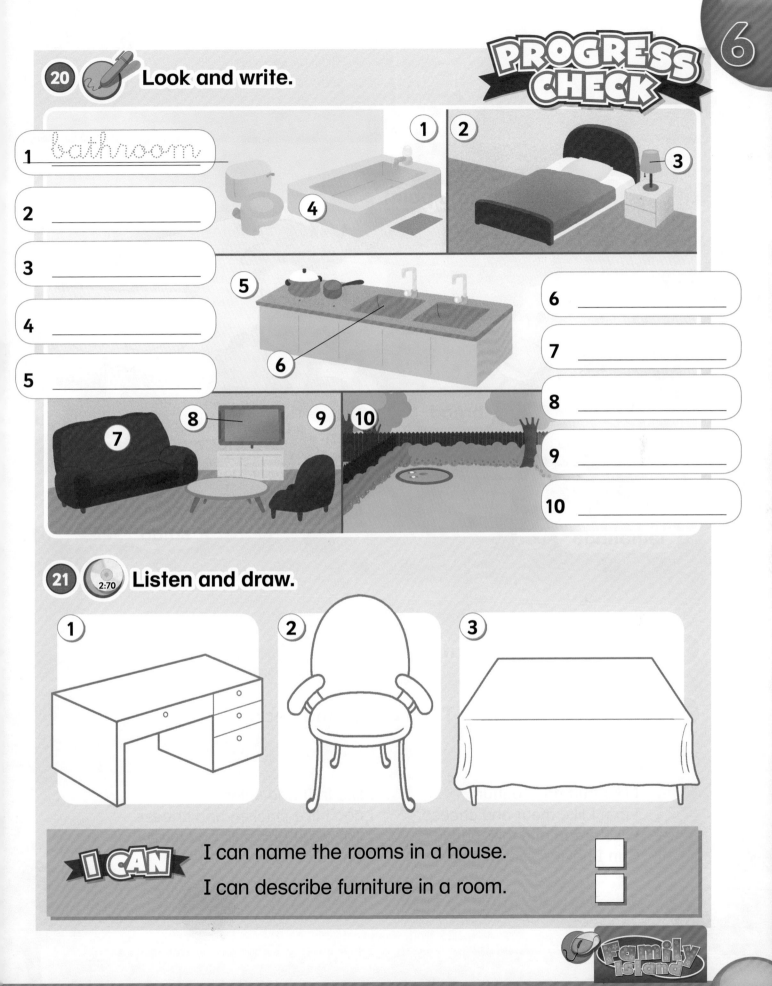

1 bathroom
2 _____
3 _____
4 _____
5 _____

6 _____
7 _____
8 _____
9 _____
10 _____

21 2:70 Listen and draw.

1

2

3

I CAN
I can name the rooms in a house.
I can describe furniture in a room.

7 Food

1 🔊 3:01 **Listen and point.**

cheese

bread

chicken

meat

juice

lemonade

salad

2 🔊 3:02 **Listen and repeat.**

3 🔊 3:03 **Listen and play. Then listen and chant.**

I like fruit and yoghurt.
I don't like meat and cheese.
I like bread and milk and juice.
Can I have some, please?

I like fruit and salad.
I don't like chicken and cheese.
I like meat and milk and juice.
Can I have some, please?

LOOK!

I like salad and meat.
I don't like bread and cheese.

| What do you want? | I want milk. |

don't = do not

yoghurt

milk

fruit

4 3:04 **Listen and match. Then ask and answer.**

Yoghurt

I like yoghurt.
What do you want?

I want milk and fruit.

3:05

Quest

Look for milk today.
An egg, a blanket, a book, a photo,
soap, a mouse, a bed and milk!
Look for milk today!

5 3:06 **Listen and repeat.**

a  **sandwich**

b **water**

c **chocolate**

d **honey**

e **jelly**

f **vegetables**

g **ice cream**

h **cake**

6 3:07 **Listen and write. Then sing and act.**

SONG

I like ___jelly___. It's nice and sweet!
I like _____. It's good to eat!

I like _____. But I don't like _____.
I like _____. But I don't like bees!
Yes, I like _____.
But I don't like bees. (x3)

Cut-outs
p.115

7 3:09 **Listen and write (✓) or (✗).**
Then ask and answer.

LOOK!

| Do you like honey? | Yes, I do. |
| | No, I don't. |

Ellie	✓					
Me						
My friend						

Do you like honey?

Yes, I do.

8 3:10 **Listen and guess.**

SKILLS

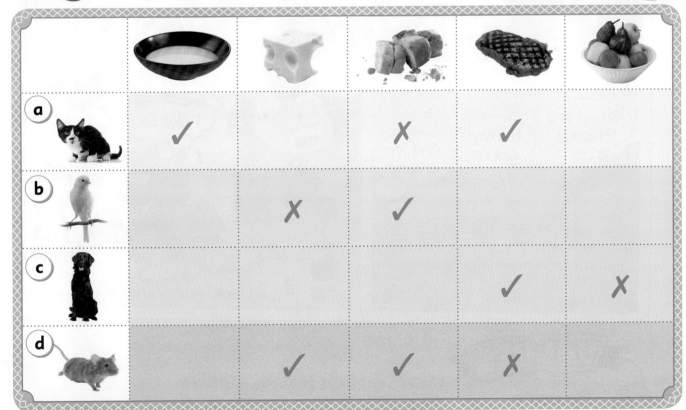

a		✓		✗	✓	
b			✗	✓		
c					✓	✗
d		✓	✓	✗		

 **Listen.**

1 **j** **2** **ss** **3** **v** **4** **w**

11 **Listen, point and say.**

12 **Listen and blend the sounds.**

1 j - a - m jam **2** j - e - t jet

3 k - i - ss kiss **4** m - e - ss mess

5 v - a - n van **6** v - e - t vet

7 w - e - b web **8** w - i - g wig

13 **Underline _j_, _ss_, _v_ and _w_. Read the words aloud.**

1 jet

2 wig

3 kiss

4 web

5 van

6 jam

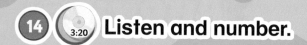

14 3:20 **Listen and number.**

a [ ] sausages

b [ ] chips

c [1] carrots

CLIL

15 **Tick (✓) the foods that are good for you. Then say.**

I like salad. It's good for me.

I like chocolate. But it's bad for me.

1 [✓] 2 [ ] 3 [ ] 4 [ ]

5 [ ] 6 [ ] 7 [ ] 8 [ ]

MINI-PROJECT
Make a food poster.

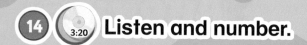

76 Lesson 7 social sciences (food)

AB p.74

Wider World

Packed lunches

16 **Read and match.**

1

I've got sandwiches and fruit.
I've got a yoghurt. I like
yoghurt but I don't like jelly. I
like milk but I don't like juice.

2

I've got bread and cheese and
salad. I like salad but I don't
like fruit. I like chocolate. I like
juice but I don't like milk.

3

I've got sushi! It's fish and rice.
I've got fruit and I've got a
cake. I don't like juice or milk.
I've got water to drink.

4

I've got chicken and vegetables.
I don't like bread. I like juice.
And I like chocolate. I don't like
milk and I don't like yoghurt.

a
b
c
d

17 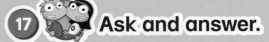 **Ask and answer.**

Do you like
sandwiches?

Do you have a
packed lunch?

What do you like
for lunch?

MINI-PROJECT
Draw a lunch
box and write.

18   **Listen. Then play and draw or .**

I don't like jelly.

19 **Listen and act.**

3:23

Picture Dictionary

AB p.110

20 3:24 Listen and circle.

1 a

b

2 a

b

3 a

b

4 a

b

5 a

b

6 a

b

21 Draw and write.

☺ fruit   I _____.

☺ bread   I _____.

☺ ice cream   I _____.

☺ vegetables I _____.

 I can name the food that I like or don't like. ☐

I can talk about food that is good for me. ☐

8 I'm excited!

1 🔘 3:26 **Listen and point.**

thirsty

scared

hungry

2 🔘 3:27 **Listen and repeat.**

3 🔘 3:28 **Listen and play. Then listen and chant.**

Are you hungry, hungry, hungry?
Are you hungry? No, I'm not!

Are you thirsty, thirsty, thirsty?
Are you thirsty? No, I'm not!

Are you tired, tired, tired?
Are you tired? No, I'm not!

Are you scared, scared, scared?
Are you scared? No, I'm not!

Are you excited, excited, excited?
Are you excited? Yes, I am!

LOOK!

| Are you hungry? | Yes, I am.
No, I'm not. |

tired

excited

3:31

Quest

Look for a torch today.
An egg, a blanket, a book,
a photo, soap, a mouse,
a bed, milk and a torch!
Look for a torch today!

4 3:30 **Listen and number. Then ask and answer.**

a b c d e

Are you excited?

Yes, I am.

You're Rita!

Yes!

5 **3:33** **Listen and repeat.**

a happy

b sad

c cold

d hot

e ill

f hurt

g angry

h bored

6 **3:34** **Listen and write. Then sing and act out.**

SONG

5, 4, 3, 2, 1

I'm happy and _excited_ .

Let's have fun!

Clap your hands.
Stamp your feet.
Click your fingers.
Drink and eat.

5, 4, 3, 2, 1

I'm _____ and excited.

Let's have fun!

Wiggle your toes.
Jump up and down.
Jump, jump, jump,
Now turn around.

5, 4, 3, 2, 1

Now, I'm tired. I'm _____ . Good night!

Cut-outs
p.117

7 **Listen and circle. Then ask and answer.**

LOOK!

Is he/she cold?	Yes, he/she is.
	No, he/she isn't. He's/She's hurt.
Are they bored?	Yes, they are.
	No, they aren't. They're excited.

aren't = are not

1

bored / excited

2

hot / cold

3

happy / sad

8 **Play a guessing game. Ask and answer.**

1

2

3

4

5

6

Are they thirsty?

No, they aren't.

Are they hurt?

Yes, they are.

Number 6!

VALUES

 Respect feelings.
Help others.

HOME-SCHOOL LINK

Help someone in your family. Take care of your younger and older family members.

10 🔊 3:38 **Listen.**

¹ **qu**   ² **x**   ³ **y**   ⁴ **z**   ⁵ **zz**

11 🔊 3:39 **Listen, point and say.**

12 🔊 3:40 **Listen and blend the sounds.**

1 qu - i - z quiz   2 qu - i - ck quick

3 b - o - x box   4 t - a - x - i taxi

5 y - e - s yes   6 y - e - ll yell

7 z - a - p zap   8 z - i - p zip

9 b - u - zz buzz   10 f - i - zz fizz

13 ✏️ **Underline _qu_, _x_, _y_, _z_ and _zz_.**

1 zip   2 taxi   3 buzz

4 yes   5 quiz   6 box

      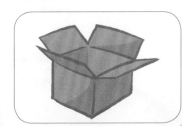

a a long shadow ☐

b a short shadow ☐

15 ✏️ **Match and say.**

1

2

3

4

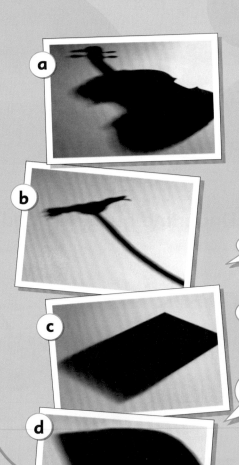

a

b

c

d

What's this?

Is it a book?

No, it isn't. It's cheese!

MINI-PROJECT
Make a shadows puzzle album!

Wider World

Shadow puppets

16 **Read and match.**

a This shadow puppet is from Indonesia. She's a dancer!

b This puppet is a house. How many windows can you see?

c These puppets are pets! There is a cat and a dog.

d This shadow puppet is from China. It's a dragon!

1

2

3

4

MINI-PROJECT
Have a shadow puppet show!

17  **Look and number. Then make a shadow puppet.**

a Cut.

b Stick.

c Look at puppet.

d Draw.

START →

He's scared.

He's got clean hands.

He doesn't like chicken.

Picture Dictionary

19 3:47 **Listen and act.**

AB p.111

20 3:49 **Listen and tick (✓). Then write.**

bored happy scared ~~thirsty~~

1
a  ✓
b

I'm _____*thirsty*_____.

2
a
b

He's _____.

3
a
b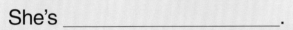

She's _____.

4
a
b

They're _____.

21 **Look at Activity 20. Read and answer.**

1 Look at number 2a. Is he scared? ___*Yes, he is.*___

2 Look at number 3b. Is she sad? _____

3 Look at number 4a. Are they cold? _____

 I can ask and talk about feelings. ☐

I can talk about shadows and light. ☐

Goodbye

1 🔘 3:50 **Listen and find.**

2 🔘 3:51 **Listen and number.**

a [ ]

b **DRAGONS** [ ]

c [ ]

d [ ]

e [ ]

f [ ]

g [ ]

h [ ]

i [1]

 ③ **Find and point. Then play *True* or *False* with a friend.**

His name's Rita.

False!

There's a blanket.

True!

Waldo is sad.

False!

4 🔘 3:52 **Look and find six differences. Then listen and check.**

1 **2**

In picture 1, he's happy.

In picture 2, he's sad.

5 ✏️ **Look at picture 2. Read and match.**

1 Has she got blue shoes?

a It's on the chair.

2 How many sandwiches can you see?

b No, he hasn't.

3 Is he happy?

c Yes, she has.

4 Where is the frog?

d Four.

5 Has he got a parrot?

e No, he isn't.

6 **3:54** **Listen and sing.** **SONG**

Come with us, come on a quest,
Come on a quest today!
Come with us, come on a quest,
Come on a quest today!

An egg, a blanket, a book, a photo, soap,
a mouse, a bed, milk and a torch …
We've got them all today.

Waldo's with his mum and dad.
Wave goodbye! Don't be sad.
Waldo's with his mum and dad.
Wave goodbye! Don't be sad.
Goodbye! Goodbye! Goodbye!
Goodbye! Goodbye! Goodbye!

7 **Draw and colour. Then write.**

Food	School object	Pet

8 **Show a friend.**
Ask and answer.

Is it a bird?   Yes, it is.

Halloween

1 **Listen, find and say.**

monster

witch

cat

pumpkin

bat

2 **Listen and sing.**

3 **Make a pumpkin and play.**

It's Halloween, it's Halloween,
Pass the pumpkin, 1, 2, 3.
Pass the pumpkin to me!

I'm a monster. I'm a bat.
I'm a pumpkin. I'm a witch, ha, ha, ha!
And I've got a cat.

It's Halloween, it's Halloween,
Pass the pumpkin, 1, 2, 3.
Pass the pumpkin to me!

Christmas

1 **3:57** **Listen, find and say.**

Santa

present

reindeer

sleigh

2 **3:58** **Listen and sing.**

3 **Make a Christmas card for your family.**

It's Christmas Day (x2),
Here comes Santa in his sleigh!
It's Christmas Day (x2),
Santa's on his way.

Look at the reindeer, 1, 2, 3.
Look at the presents. Can you see?
Red, yellow, green and blue,
Orange, pink and purple, too!

It's Christmas Day...
Happy Christmas!

Happy Christmas!

Easter

1 **Listen, find and say.**

egg

chick

bunny

2 **Listen and sing.**

3 **Make an Easter egg. Have an egg hunt!**

It's Easter time,
Time for fun.

Can you see the chicks
Go cheep, cheep, cheep?
Can you see the bunny
Go hop, hop, hop?
Can you see the eggs
For you and me, you and me?

Find, find, find, find the chicks,
Find, find, find, find the bunny,
Find, find, find, find the eggs.

It's Easter time,
Time for fun
Happy Easter everyone!

Summer fun

1 **Listen, find and say.**

sky · bird · tree · sun · flower · grass

2 **Listen and chant.**

3 **Make and play.**

It's summer time,
Come out and play.
At summer camp,
We play all day.

The grass is green,
The trees are, too.
The flowers are red,
And the sky is blue.

It's summer time…

The birds are happy.
They sing in the sun.
And we are happy.
Summer camp is fun!

Grammar reference

Welcome

Names and identifying characters:

Hello. My name's Oscar.

I'm Oscar.

His name's Oscar.

His backpack is red.

Her name's Millie.

Her backpack is green.

name's = name is

Imperatives:

Stand up! Sit down!

Unit 1

Personal questions:

What's your name?

How old are you?

What's your favourite colour?

What's = What is

My name's Millie.

I'm seven.

My favourite colour is green.

I'm = I am

Asking about colours (singular objects):

Is it purple?

What colour is it?

It's = It is

Yes, it is./No, it isn't.

It's pink.

Isn't = Is not

Unit 2

Identifying objects (singular and plural):

What's this?

What are these?

They're = They are

It's a book. It's red. It's a red book.

They're pencils.

Asking about colours (plural objects):

What colour are they?

They're red.

How many pencils can you see?

Five.

Unit 3

Introducing family members:
This is my brother/sister.

Asking and answering about age:

How old is he/she?   He's/She's nine.

He's/She's = He is/She is

Asking and answering about occupations (short answers):

Is he/she a dancer?   Yes, he/she is.
Is he/she an artist?   No, he/she isn't. He's/She's a cook.

Unit 4

Talking about possession:

I've got a green tail.   I've got green wings.
He's got blue trousers.   She's got a yellow head.
She's got four legs. They're purple.

I've got = I have got   He's/She's got = He/She has got

Unit 5

Identifying objects from far away:

What's that?	It's a dog.
What are those?	They're hamsters.

Asking and answering about possession (short answers):

Have you got a parrot?	Yes, I have. It's a small parrot.
	No, I haven't.
Has he/she got a parrot?	Yes, she has. It's a small parrot.
	No, he hasn't. He's got a big dog.

haven't = have not   hasn't = has not

Unit 6

Asking and answering about location:

Where's Rita?	She's in the kitchen.
Where are Waldo and Zak?	They're in the bedroom.

Where's = Where is

Describing a room:

There's a lamp on the desk.   There are two kittens under the sofa.

There's = There is

Unit 7

Expressing likes and dislikes with food:

I like salad and meat.   I don't like bread and cheese.

don't = do not

Asking and answering about food choices:

What do you want?   I want milk.

Asking and answering about likes and dislikes:

Do you like honey?   Yes, I do./No, I don't.

Unit 8

Expressing emotion:

I'm hungry.   He's/She's thirsty.

Asking and answering about emotions (short answers):

Are you hungry?   Yes, I am./No, I'm not.

Is he/she cold?   Yes, he is.

No, she isn't. She's hurt.

Are they bored?   Yes, they are.

No, they aren't. They're excited.

aren't = are not

What can you do in English? Ask and say. Then tick (✓).

Can you say your name? ☐

Can you say your age? ☐

Can you name six colours? ☐

Can you say your favourite colour? ☐

Can you count to twenty? ☐

Can you name five school objects? ☐

Can you name four musical instruments? ☐

Can you describe your family? ☐

Can you name five jobs? ☐

Can you name six parts of the body? ☐

Can you name five items of clothing? ☐

Can you name the rooms in a house? ☐

Can you describe the furniture in your bedroom? ☐

Can you describe your classroom? ☐

Can you name seven animals? ☐

Can you say the food you like? ☐

Can you say the food you don't like? ☐

Can you name two food items that are bad for you? ☐

Can you say how you are feeling today? ☐

Pearson Education Limited
Edinburgh Gate
Harlow
Essex CM20 2JE
England
and Associated Companies throughout the world.

www.islands.pearson.com

© Pearson Education Limited 2012

Stories on pages 14, 24, 34, 44, 54, 64, 74 and 84 by Steve Elsworth and Jim Rose. The rights of Steve Elsworth and Jim Rose to be identified as authors of this work have been asserted by them in accordance with the Copyright, Designs and Patents Act 1988.

All rights reserved; no part of this publication may be reproduced, stored in a retrieval system, or transmitted in any form or by any means, electronic, mechanical, photocopying, recording, or otherwise without the prior written permission of the Publishers.

First published 2012
Seventh impression 2018
ISBN: 978-1-4479-03116

Based on the work of Tessa Lochowski, Laura Miller and José Luis Morales

Illustrators: Leo cultura, Joelle Dreidemy (Bright Agency), Marek Jagucki, Sue King (Plum Pudding Illustration), Stephenine Lau, Yam Wai Lun, Katie McDee, Bill McGuire (Shannon Associates), Jackie Stafford, Olimpia Wong, and Teddy Wong

Set in Fiendstar 17/21pt
Printed in Slovakia by Neografia

Picture Credits
The Publisher would like to thank the following for their kind permission to reproduce their photographs:

(Key: b-bottom; c-centre; l-left; r-right; t-top)

Alamy Images: ACE STOCK LIMITED 27 (3), Agencja FREE 76 (a), Alex Segre 66b (a), Alistair Laming 66t (c), avatra images 27 (Alex), Bill Gozansky 26 (d), Chris Mattison 57 (d), Chuck Franklin 12 (h), Corbis Super RF 26 (a), Ellen Isaacs 86t (b), J Marshall - Tribaleye Images 67 (3), Jeff Morgan 07 27 (1), Justin Leighton 27 (4), Ken Welsh 67 (d), Lebrecht Music and Arts Photo Library 26 (b), Mark Richardson 67 (b), Meridian Images 89 (4b), nobleIMAGES 67 (2), Powered by Light / Alan Spencer 56 (3), Yuri Arcurs 12 (f); **Corbis:** Jim Craigmyle 66b (b), Martyn Rose 27 (2); **DK Images:** Steve Shott 17 (2); **Fotolia.com:** Africa Studio 57 (c), Anatoliy Samara 17 (5), Anyka 12 (b), fivespots 57b (snake), Ilia Shcherbakov 57b (rat), Ivonne Wierink 17 (4), Jacek Chabraszewski 12 (a), 12 (e), Jacek Chabraszewski 12 (a), 12 (e), jonnysek 57b (rabbit), Lana Langlois 57b (lizard), NIK 57b (tortoise), Olga Sapegina 12 (d), Pixel Memoirs 57 (a), Rafael Ramirez 39 (8b), Scott Waby 57b (spider), Sergey Lavrentev 76 (c), Sergii Figurnyi 57b (goldfish), 57b (mouse), SergiyN 8 (c), Werg 57 (b), YellowCrest 67 (a); **Getty Images:** Alistair Berg 66b (c), Stone / Mary Kate Denny 27 (5); **iStockphoto:** ac-bnphotos 76 (6), Alexander Ishchenko 73 (d), Andy Gehrig 16 (a), Beverley Vycital 16 (1), Derek Dammann 16 (d), Eric Isselee 16 (4), 73 (b), 73 (c), futureimage 26 (1), Gennady Kudelya 16 (b), Gustavo Andrade 76 (7), jerryhat 76 (1), Joe Gough 73 (steak), Jorge Farres Sanchez 73 (bread), Josef Muellek 76 (8), juanmonino 76 (2), 76 (4), juanmonino 76 (2), 76 (4), Katarzyna Leszczynska 12 (g), Liz Leyden 16 (e), Michael Shabtai 76cl, Petr Koudelka 16 (5), pixhook 26 (3), 26 (4), Sean Locke 67 (4), Stephen Morris 73 (fruit); **Pearson Education Ltd:** Trevor Clifford 8 (a), 8 (b), 8 (d), 8 (e), 8 (f), 8 (g), 8 (h), 12 (c); **Pearson Education Ltd:** Trevor Clifford 46, 49, 57 (Angela), 57 (boy & girl), 57 (Grace), 67 (1), 86 (1,2,3,4,a,b,c,d), 94, 95, 96, Eyewire 26 (2), jupiterimages 76 (5), MindStudio 57 (Matt), Photodisc. Neil Beer 67 (c), Photodisc. Photolink 17 (3), Studio 8 57 (Ben), Trevor Clifford 46, 49, 57 (Angela), 57 (boy & girl), 57 (Grace), 67 (1), 86 (1,2,3,4,a,b,c,d), 94, 95, 96; **Photolibrary. com:** Bilderlounge 17 (1), 79 (1a), Ingram Publishing 26 (c), Juniors Bildarchiv 56b (a), 56b (b), Oxford Scientific (OSF) / Elliot Neep 56b (c), STOCK4B-RF 76 (b), Stockbroker 89 (4a); **RSPB Images:** Mark Sisson 56c (a); **Shutterstock.com:** 13l, Adrian Hughes 82 (e), Ajay Bhaskar 39 (4b), Alexander Raths 39 (1b), Amlet 79 (5b), Andrea Leone 62 (a), Anneka 59 (1a), Apollofoto 43, Catalin Petolea 63, Cheryl Casey 66b (d), Dan Peretz 79 (5a), Dan70 16 (c), Danny Smythe 79 (2b), David Davis 89 (1b), Drozdowski 79 (6b), Eric Isselee 56 (1), 59 (1b), 59 (5b), Erik Lam 56c (c), EuToch 62 (f), Excellent backgrounds 62 (h), Feng Yu 79 (2a), Filip Fuxa 16 (2), 66t (f), Flashon Studio 39 (7a), Galina Barskaya 86t (a), Gelpi 23l, 82 (g), Giuseppe_R 89 (3b), Hannamariah 73 (a), Ingret 59 (6b), IntraClique LLC 89 (2a), J. McPhail 82 (h), Jan Martin Will 59 (5a), John McLaird 89 (1a), Jorg Hackemann 82 (d), Jules Studio 33l, Junial Enterprises 23r, Juriah Mosin 89 (3a), Kamira 76cr, Leah-Anne Thompson 82 (f), Ledo 79 (4a), Lepas 79 (3a), Liv Friis-Larsen 82 (c), Ljupco Smokovski 62 (d), Marc Dietrich 73 (cheese), Marco Mayer 79 (3b), Monika Wisniewska 39 (3a), Monkey Business Images 39 (5b), newphotoservice 66t (b), Nicolas McComber 39 (5a), Noam Armonn 79 (1b), OlgaLis 73 (milk), olly 39 (4a), Omers 62 (c), Paul Matthew Photography 82 (a), Perry Correl 79 (4b), Pete Saloutos 39 (6a), Phil Date 39 (1a), ppart 62 (b), R.Iegosyn 59 (6b), Ragne Kabanova 66t (d), RealDealPhoto / Bobby Deal 39 (7b), Rob Byron 79 (6a), Rohit Seth 33r, Sandra van der Steen 82 (b), Smolych Iryna 66t (e), Studiots 62 (e), Subbotina Anna 59 (2a), Terekhov Igor 62 (g), Terri Francis 66t (a), Timofey 39 (3b), 39 (8a), Tissiana Bowman 59 (6a), Tony Wear 59 (2b), Viktorl 76 (3), WilleeCole 56 (2), Yuri Arcurs 13r, 39 (2a), 39 (2b), Yuri Arcurs 13r, 39 (2a), 39 (2b), Yuri Arcurs 13r, 39 (2a), 39 (2b), Zurijeta 89 (2b); **Thinkstock:** Brand X Pictures 16 (3), Hemera 56c (b)

Every effort has been made to trace the copyright holders and we apologise in advance for any unintentional omissions. We would be pleased to insert the appropriate acknowledgment in any subsequent edition of this publication.

All other images © Pearson Education Ltd

Illustration Acknowledgements

Moreno Chiacchiera (Beehive Illustration), Joelle Dreidemy (Bright Agency), HL Studios, Sue King (Plum Pudding Illustration), Katie McDee, Bill McGuire (Shannon Associates), Jackie Stafford, Leo Cultura, Marek Jagucki, Stephenine Lau, Yam Wai Lun, Olimpia Wong, and Teddy Wong.

Cut and play, Unit 2, page 22.

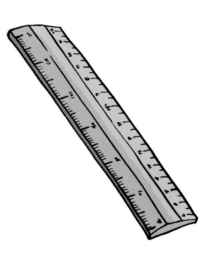

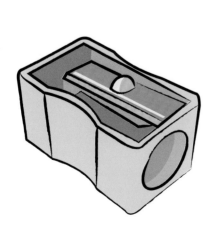

Cut and play, Unit 3, page 32.

Cut and play, Unit 4, page 42.

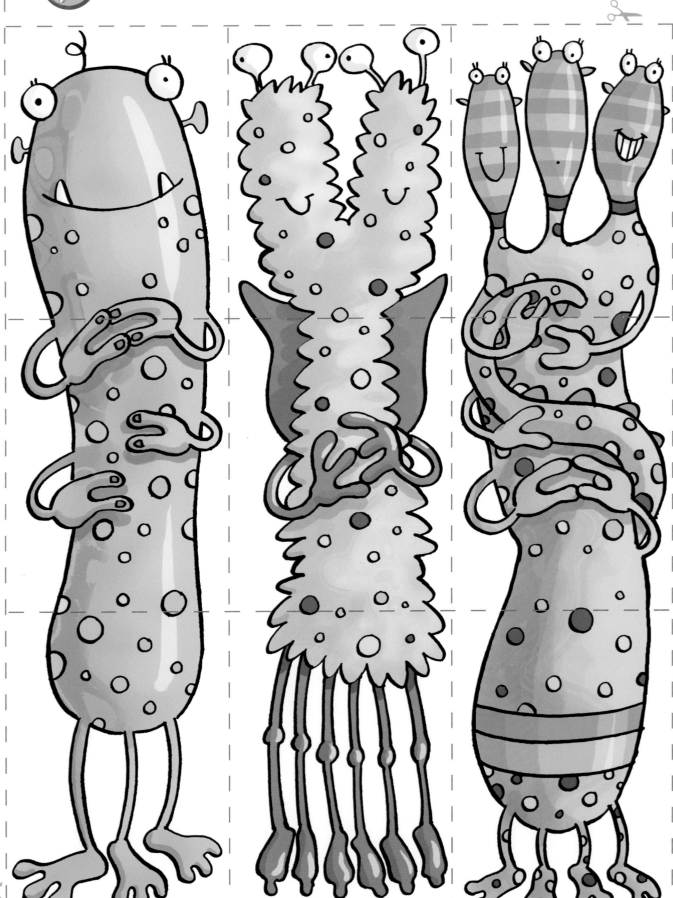

Yoghurt

HONEY